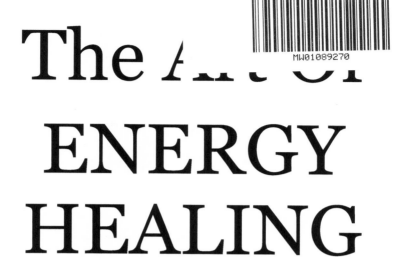

The Art of

ENERGY

HEALING

How To Channel Your Intuitive Energy
And Heal The Body, Mind & Spirit

Written By Rev. Dr. Geraldine Johnson-Carter

"Life is ENERGY and, as such, it belongs to all, reaches all, and blesses ALL."

-Donna Goddard

The information herein is offered for informational purposes solely, and is universal as so. The presentation of the information is without contract or any type of guarantee assurance.

The trademarks that are used are without any consent, and the publication of the trademark is without permission or backing by the trademark owner. All trademarks and brands within this book are for clarifying purposes only and are the owned by the owners themselves, not affiliated with this document.

Contents

WHAT IS ENERGY HEALING?

Energy healing isn't by any means a new practice. Indeed different variations of the art dates back through thousands upon thousands of years from one edge of the globe to the other. These practices have managed to make their way into mainstream America, as well as just about every industrialized nation on the planet. Today, energy healing encompasses a broad territory, with many individual schools of thought.

According to www.eastendhealth.com energy healing "addresses the subtle energy" that governs the physical body. Working directly with the emotional, mental and spiritual dimensions of this energy body, the healer affects the healing and release of blocked and distorted energy patterns enabling the innate intelligence to operate freely, restoring physical mental and spiritual health.

Since has proven that one component all living and non-living things share is energy. Human beings are also governed by this force. And though each individual's energy system is unique, the system as a whole is much the same from person to person. The main focuses of the system are known as chakras, and there are SEVEN of them.

Energy healers serve as the instrument through which the energy system is re-balanced. Through their extensive knowledge of how the human energy system functions, they are able to identify blockages and imbalances and help the "patient" get realigned and back into the proper state-of-mind.

Once restored to the proper balance, the blockages- which are the root cause of physical, mental, emotional and spiritual problems of many forms, are dissolved and well-being is returned.

The way healers go about accomplishing this is as unique as the healers themselves. Some of the most prominent variations of energy healing include:

- ✓ Reiki
- ✓ Radiant healing
- ✓ Hands –on healing
- ✓ Healing Touch

✓ Therapeutic touch

WHAT SITUATIONS WILL ENERGY HEALING WORK FOR?

Whether a person suffers from chronic physical pain and painful emotional scars, energy healing can work. Whether a person is at the height of wellness or the depth of depression or disease, they can benefit from energy healing. Male or female, young or old, without "conventional medicine" energy healing holds the power to make monumental positive changes in your life and the lives of those around you. There are many time that energy healing can be used to improve a situation. Some of them might surprise you! Energy healing can be used:

- ✓ On you by your self
- ✓ By someone else on you
- ✓ On your friends and family members
- ✓ On animals

✓ On the environment

✓ Across long distances

CAN I HEAL?

The first thing that anyone should understand about healing is that healing, in one capacity or another is inherent to human nature. The desire to minimize pain and suffering and to help others be nurtured and grow is innate. You only have to accept this fact and begin looking inward to identify your own natural abilities.

However, though the ability to heal is inherent the methods and degrees of healing aren't even countable. There are infinite possibilities when it comes to healing. However, there are some "qualifications" that are shared among successful energy healing practitioners. Some of those skills and qualifications they share include.

- A dedication to perfecting the art of healing

- A desire to increase communications skills

- A belief and acceptance of higher states of consciousness

- The ability to practice relaxation and meditation techniques

- A capacity for guided imagery and creative visualization

- Strong intuitive abilities

- Compassion

- Good listening skills (even when no one is talking)

But more than any of these things, you must have the ultimate goal of self-improvement, for it is only when you are at peak performance that you can hope to help bring others to their own optimal states.

COMMON REASONS PEOPLE DECIDE TO HEAL

#1. They have be healed themselves and liberated from the bonds of imbalanced energy, disease or illness. This is a powerful motivator for personal growth and enhances the desire to share that freedom with others.

#2. They are aware of a Natural Healing Ability. Another reason a person might be lead to the vocation of becoming a healer is because they have noticed that they have a natural healing ability. While this ability and capacity might manifest itself in various ways in different people, some are better able to recognize a propensity. Whether they are natural nurturers, actual "healers" or simply empathetic by nature, these people are able to recognize the spark and run with it.

#3. Curiosity – while perhaps not as admirable as other motives, curiosity is just as powerful. As our big world has shrunk down into a global village, we have better access to traditional medicines and therapies that are attractive in their effectiveness and in their difference. Therapies like Yoga, Reiki, Chrystal therapy and other indigenous treatments are showing greater results and attracting much more attention from mainstream publications and journals. This attention is attracting pioneering minds and individual to get involved in the best new therapies around.

#4. Frequent Exposure to Healing and Healers – Familiarity doesn't always breed contempt sometimes it breeds interest and passion. Men and women who are members of families of healers or energy therapists or other parts of the alternative medicine world or have friends or colleagues related to the industry often find it quite natural to work in this field themselves.

Energy healing and religion - While some variants of energy healing may include religion or worship, the actual practice of energy healing is available to anyone, regardless of race, sex, religion or any other factor. To become a successful energy healer, there is no need to join a particular church or ashram. Energy healing is a discipline, a practice. It's a path, designed to help improve people's lives in this life, not the life beyond the veil of death. Though it is not a religion it is an art that seems to be shared among several important religious figures such as Jesus, Buddha and Krishna, saints, apostles and other religious gurus all though out the expanse of recorded history.

THE WORKINGS OF ENERGY AND HOW TO SENSE IT
HOW DOES ENERGY WORK?

All things have energy, both living and inanimate. It is both used and stored, a solid, a liquid or a gas. It exist within our plane and without in the depths of the Universe. Energy courses through power lines and is radiated by a single, non-descript stone. But there are some differences in the way energy functions outside of us and the way that it works within us. To understand how we process our energy, it's important that we understand the makeup of the human energy system.

THE HUMAN ENERGY SYSTEM – As complex as it's workings are, understanding the basic components and functions of the human energy system is actually quite simple. Your energy system and the energy system of all humans have seven centers known as chakras. As energy flows through each of your centers in your system, it creates different experiences within your body.

THE SEVEN CHAKRAS – The seventh chakra is located in the crown of your head, it is through this point that energy enters into your energy system. It is your connection to the nonphysical Universe.

The sixth chakra can be found in your forehead, in between your eyes. This is the center of your institution, and is often referred to as the "third eye." It is through this center that you "see" more than your five senses can ever show you. It allows you to recognize opportunities for spiritual growth.

The fifth chakra can be found in the vicinity of the throat. It is related to your voice sensations in your neck and throat (such as stress, tension or even complete relaxation). Etc. It is from its center that your "voice" emanated your communication and your public representation of yourself.

The fourth Chakra is located inside of your chest. This center is essentially the "heart" of your energy system. It's the hallway that leads the centers above it to the centers below it. It is also here that you experience "heartache." It is also where you can radiate warmth and compassion, connecting with the greater world around you.

The third chakra can be found in what is known as the solar plexus. The solar plexus can be found just an inch or two superior to the navel and just inferior to the diaphragm/ribs. The place where these parts come together is about the center of your chest. It is here that you feel sensations in the "pit of your stomach." It is also where we experience "butterflies." On the flip-side, it is also the core of your confidence and competence. It is the focus point for our power and will. Our sense of power, ego and authority, as well as self-control and discipline are centered here.

The second chakra is located within the reproductive region, and is the center most frequently associated with sex and passion. However, it is much more than that it is the center and seat of your creativity.

Imbalances can result in creating ways to exploit circumstances or others. Balance leads to meaningful, mutually satisfying relationships.

The first and final chakra is located at the base of your trunk, near the genital region. This center serves as your connection to the Earth. It ties your energy systems to the energy of the world around you. It is here where our comfort and contentment with our earthly lives is rooted. Just as the seventh chakra connects us to the Universal Energy Source, our first chakra binds us to the Earth Energy Source. Charkas blockages are related to disease and illness, and balancing the overall energy systems can help release blockages.

What are Meridians When it comes to our energy systems, working in conjunction with chakras are very important avenue known as meridians. Meridians are the channels that carry the flow of energy through the body. There are twelve major energies that exist through our physical body, from the top of our head to the tips of your toes. Take a look at a color chart of the Meridians Diagram of the major body Meridians.

Understanding the Aura in order to properly grasp the concept of the aura, it is important to understand a fairly simple principle. When you are dealing with energy, you must remember that energy doesn't emanate from a person, that energy is that person core, their life force. Really "getting" this concept is absolutely fundamental to being able to maintain your energy. You must remember that energy doesn't emanate from a person that energy is that person their core, their life force. Really "getting" this concept is absolutely fundamental to being able to maintain your energy field and your body in harmony with one another.

Because our bodies are a manifestation of human energy, any time there is a dissonance within our energy field, disease is a natural result. Anytime our energy fields are out of whack, our physical bodies will also become imbalanced. The personality there are three main components of the personality, through the number of possible resulting combinations is infinite. The three main components are the basic self, the conscious self, and the higher self.

Our basic selves are in charge of our body functions, memories and our survival instinct. It is also here that you will find a person's belief system. It contains our ingrained family patterns, social norms the pattern of our destiny, "our inner" and our will to survive. Habits are rooted here too. Our basic self is under the authority of our conscious self, but is entirely capable of lying to you when your consciousness is trying to hide from the truth. Many people have multiple basic selves which allow them to view the world through various perspectives.

The conscious self is made up of our waking lives and is responsible for creating new awareness. It is both creative and innocent until a choice has been set in motion. The conscious self is made up of our waking lives and is responsible for creating new awareness. It is both creative and innocent until a choice has been set in motion. The conscious self mediates each of the three selves. We are able to extend our conscious self, and come into a better awareness of our higher self and conscious of the working of the basic self when we grow in our personal awareness and spiritual illuminations.

The higher self serves as a guardian angel of sorts. It isn't itself the source, but is very similar. The higher self isn't able to function when we suffer from low-self esteem. It is the energy of our life and our form and is both creative and non-inflicting. In fact, our high self is a spiritual form that exists in our personal consciousness and is always connected to the Spirit- the forces that are beyond our own personal domains. Our high self must be able to connect with our basic selves in order to guide us well upon the road of our destinies. However, you must remember the high self, thrush because it may have superior wisdom to offer, but it will not override our own conscious choices until we ask and allow it to. The final thing to consider regarding our personality is our soul itself. Your soul is made up of both your essential divine, nature, plus your experience.

The divine energy of the soul is formless, timeless and eternal. The Aura is a term for protecting psychic and spiritual energy field that both surrounds and penetrates our physical bodies. This is depicted in art as a halo that denotes heightened spirituality or purity. When the Bible uses the words "raiment" or "countenance of light," they are referring to the aura of the person being described. People gifted with the natural ability to detect and read the aura will often use descriptive visual phrases such as having;

- A blood mood

- Scarlet with anger

- Absolutely green with envy

- Thriving with energy

- Radiantly beautiful

This intuitive reasoning allows us to form impressions and also experience the emotions and feelings of not only ourselves, but also others. Popular yoga psychology perceives the aura as an energy field which surrounds the body and interacts via spiritual and psychological levels using our chakras. The appearance of an aura be it beautiful or repelling will depend on a great many things like.

- Physical health
- Emotion attitude and
- Spiritual development

The human aura is a complex web of the physical emotional and mind-spirit aspects of the self. It is the self manifesting itself as energy. Our experiences from our daily lives will register inside our aura in many ways including: Color, lines, dots, emanations, and/or vibrations.

Every aura is special and unique, and the hidden self is expressed here. By learning to read and sense energy by studying the aura, it is possible to gain a very intimate insight into the overall energy of a person – even things they are not aware of themselves.

THE LEVELS OF THE AURA

It is a widely held belief that the human aura is made up of seven major levels that are broken down into three different regions. The seven major levels are:

- The archetypal aura

- The spiritual aura

- The mental aura

- The emotional aura

- The imaginable aura

- The etheric aura

- The physical aura

The mental, archetypal and spiritual auras extend the farthest, reaching out about three feet from the body.

It encompasses all of the other levels. The imaginable and emotional auras emanate about two feet from the body and envelope the physical and etheric levels. The physical and etheric levels reach about six inches to about a foot.

THE PHYSICAL AURA – Physical trauma, cell memory, physical wellness, emotions and psychological beliefs are all reflected in our physical aura. These things are able to penetrate both the physical and etheric levels. When balanced, the physical aura is able to handle superior forces that lie deeper within the psyche.

THE ETHERIC AURA – Serves as a blueprint for our physical bodies. Meridians and chakras are housed at this level. It helps to create and maintain our body's form. Whenever the energy in the etheric level is blocked or moved out of balance, this imbalance will somehow manifest itself in the physical body.

THE IMAGINAL AURA – Serves as the conduit through which we both create and transform our circumstances. Many important functions of perception, including intension, positive self-image, visual learning and visualization, healing, manifestation, institution and success are generated at the imagination level. Used holistically, it can be the catalyst for connecting, integrating and aligning all levels. However, used at the expense of the other levels, it can be truly horrifying. Delusions and obsessions stem from and are reflected through this level. It is this level that is also most affected by alcohol and substance abuse. Drugs separate your from your capability to fulfill your soul's purpose, offering a counterfeit or escapism process instead of facing the challenges and rewards that are your true calling.

THE EMOTIONAL AURA – This is where we carry the relics of our feelings as well as our emotional actions and reactions. This is the source of our drive for power, dominance and our competitive natures. However, it is also the root of our passion and ability to embrace love, heal and forgive. More than any other level, this is our own personal peace maker.

THE MENTAL AURA – In this level of the aura we build our relationship to our destinies and inner levels. Our beliefs and attitudes are reflected here. It is our mental activities that build our internal structure and is where and how we project ourselves into our lives. This is where our reality is shaped and shaded. Generally, mental health (or, mental illness) is mirrored on this level.

THE SPIRITUAL AURA – Of our aura is where we reflect our magnificent nature, our divine spark onto our social, psychological and physical realities. This level reflects (and responds) to the balance and alignment of all of the other levels too. As the aura as a whole becomes more balanced, this level becomes more pronounced.

THE ACHETYPAL AURA – At this level is found the map or your individual destiny. A master to-do list that provides you with tasks and obstacles it is your fate to surmount and accomplish. It is our soul curriculum, if you will. We came into our physical lives with an internal, archetypal lesson plan. This plan is rooted in our subconscious self.

THE AURA AS AN ENERGY HEALING AID – When it comes to learning to sense another person's energy, learning to discern and read the aura is perhaps one of the most powerful visual methods you will have at your disposal. While some re naturally gifted with the ability to see the auras of others, if you are not you should not despair. It is possible to train yourself to see and read the human aura. It is important to find a method that provides you with the most desirable results.

SENSING ENERGY IN THE CHAKRAS AND THE AURA – CREATIVE VISUALIZATION –allows you to see the aura or chakra in your mind.

MEDITATION – allows you to gain insight into the aura and chakras is done by clearing your mind and using deep relaxing breathing to help center yourself and allow the person's energy field to manifest itself before you.

PRACTICE – is a surefire way to make progress in sensing another person's energy field. The more you immerse yourself in the art of sensing another person's energy field, the more real and apparent it will become to you.

GO TO: www.chosehealing.com – This site breaks down the healing process into a total of three levels, each more advanced than the other. For exercises related to sensing the aura or chakras, visit Chios Healing Level II and navigate the tool bar to the left of the screen for additional exercises and insights into this amazing ability.

OTHER WAYS TO SENSE ENERGY

- The laying on of hands,

- Biofeedback

- Emotional response diagnostics

- Intuition

- Various different technical energy reading devices

It is important for the healer to understand that you are not doing the healing, but instead you are serving as a vessel through which the patient learns to heal and balance themselves. Coming to terms with this fact early on is vital to keeping your motives and your ego clear and open.

While many pioneers of energy healing may have felt their practice fell outside of "mainstream" medicine, now it's been determined that they have been responsible for breaking ground in an advanced and cutting edge approach of research and practice. In fact, it is a widely held opinion in the scientific community that energy healing and medicine may very well be the foundation for the next leaps and bounds in personalized health care. As evidence in favor of energy healing continues to mount, you will soon see that these energy healing practices will become accepted and part of more conventional therapies and practitioners.

Right now, one of the biggest obstacles energy healing is facing is not having a simple standardized explanation of "why" and "how" these therapies work. No one is denying that it does work but without knowing "why" or "how", it is difficult to reconstruct these therapies in clinical ways. However scientists are aware that when new therapies and theories emerge they are usually performed intuitively, long before the results have been quantified or objectified.

Energy healing is a perfect example of this situation. Many ancient arts like the laying on of hands, therapeutic touch, aura balancing, acupuncture, polarity and other various forms of the art are not just beginning to be understood within the scientific community. Widely believed theory and explanation of how energy healing works. Every ember and process that makes up our body will produce a unique set of energy fields. These fields are able to travel through your organs and tissues. But those fields don't stop there. They also extend beyond the body and into the space surrounding you – your "bubble space"!!!

Every function, every change in your body produces its own characteristic electrical current. These currents are strongest where they originate but they are also conducted into the nearby surrounding tissues. As these currents flow, a bio-magnetic field is created in the space surrounding the body. Scientists recently began paying closer attention to the concept of bio-magnetic fields with the development of a very powerful tool known as SQUID which stands for superconducting quantum interface device and its function is that of an incredible sensitive magnetometer.

It can measure the bio-magnet field given off by a single beat of the heart or a mere twitch of the toe. Using SQUID, scientists and researchers are investing great time and effort to map the powerful energy fields that surround our bodies to very precise specifications. As it sits now, even Western bio-medicine is willing to accept that disorders can be cured by introducing a field to their body. That's the principle behind pacemaker technology and the electric and magnetic devices used to aid bone fracture healing. Biologist have discovered that many living systems are incredible sensitive to field that were once considered too weak to even make an influence upon us.

Take the homing pigeon, which operates its navigations from reading the magnetic fields of the earth, as an example. While it is not yet known how great a role energy healing will play in conventional medicine there is a growing trend to use energy healing to accelerate the effectiveness of other therapies. It is believed that one reason tissue will heal slowly stems from the fact that the channels that transmit communication from the tissue to the rest of the body are performing below par. And as this communication breaks down so does the ability to heal. To experience optimal performance, you must offer a whole system solution that re-opens those lines of communication that connect organs, tissues, cells and molecules into a single network.

And while improvement may be seen for a short time by merely treating the symptoms of this dysfunction, if this core communication problem isn't cured, these symptoms are doomed to manifest themselves again at a later time. That is because for the real healing to occur, tissue that may be located some distance away from the source must also participate in the process. If the lines of communication are blocked, important messages, signals and other portions of the healing process can't get to the root of the problem.

An energy healer can remedy this situation by helping to open communication networks, or even by inserting messages that haven't been able to make it through. Obviously, by treating the root of the disorder, you help re-align your client's own natural bodily repair system. That's the role that the energy healer plays. Two recent breakthroughs in the field of cell biology that might explain why this works, the first breakthrough that was discovered is called the human semiconductor when it was found that the molecules that make up our bodies are actually semi conductors. A semiconductor is something that is able to transmit both energy and information, among other things. They also store information and process signals. They are also used, outside of the body, as an essential component of today's electronic industry.

The second breakthrough came by the way of the discovery that this intricate network extends not only across cell surfaces, but also into the interiors of these cells – even as far as the nucleus and even DNA. This matrix is known as cytoskeleton. It has been suggested that this network might be organized in such a way that is quite similar to a situation where a network of computers works together to solve a common problem. The challenge of energy healers today is to figure out the precise way a living version of this "networking".

Your actual faith will play an integral role in your ability to heal. Before you can have faith in your own ability to heal, you must first have a solid faith that healing actually works. There are numerous instances of "unexplained" healings that defy conventional medicine's "rules" and these aren't a few isolated events either. Time after time in place after place, there is a new breaking story that covers some new instance of alternative therapies gaining ground where conventional medicines were unable to.

Once you have come to terms with the fact that healing does in fact work, it is time to take another leap. As of faith and understand that separation is no obstacle to success. As long as you can make a solid connection with your client or subject, you can facilitate healing. Even if the connection is only perceived (as opposed to over the telephone or via an online conference) you can still use the connection to change and improve the performance and health of their overall energy system. Energy healing works whenever the practitioner is able to realign the clients' natural energy flow, dissolving blockages that are the root causes that various illnesses stem from. However, in order to really be able to play your role in the healing process, it helps if you have a clearer idea of what disease and illness mean in connection to your overall energy system.

MORE ABOUT DISEASE

Disease and illness are usually symptoms of an underlying disruption in the energy chakras. These blockages and disruptions interfere with the body's natural communication efforts and isolate that area from the influence of surrounding regions. When an energy healer steps into a situation like this, their primary function is to get the energy channels clear and open. This can be done with targeted regional therapies or an overall holistic approach. However, more often than not, the situation may call for both.

There are virtually and infinite number of maladies that can be improved (or often cured) using energy healing therapies such as:

1. Addictive cravings

2. Allergies

3. Anxiety/panic attacks

4. Anger

5. Obsessive behavior

6. Depression

7. Insomnia

8. Repressive memories or negative memories

9. Nightmares

10. Chronic pain

11. Physical healing

12. Grief bereavement

13. Self image repair.

Of course just about any negative manifestation of a dysfunctional energy can be corrected via energy healing from seemingly "trivial problems" to life-threatening illnesses.

NEW ENERGY PSYCHOTHERAPIES

In addition to older, more traditional therapies, recently many new therapies have been introduced that are reported to produce rapid results sometimes within only minutes! According to Dr. Fred Gallo, a leading authority on the subject, the introduction of the energy paradigm to clinical psychology as well as to other branches of psychology and psychotherapy is truly a major shift in perspective, directing our attention to an entirely unique set of variables. But within the real quantum physics, which is really the domain of subtle energy, electrons and so on, the universe does not operate as neatly as Newton has proposed.

Within this real, change can occur instantaneously without having to pass through the intermediary stages required in a Newtonian universe. It is commonly acknowledged among professional and lay public alike that most psychotherapeutic approaches do not produce therapeutic results rapidly. Frequently, extended periods of time are required before the patient is pronounced "significantly" improved but hardly ever cured. Recently several therapies have emerged that reportedly produced rapid therapeutic results, often within a matter of minutes. Indeed, these methods significantly deviate from therapies based on traditional behavioral cognitive, developmental systemic, neurologic and chemical paradigms.

Admittedly few people have any real understanding of how these therapies work, but the fact that they do, and that they work so quickly and effectively, has drawn greater conventional attention. Energy and meridian therapies where introduced to us back in 1964 by a chiropractor by the name of George Goodhear, the founder of the applied kinesiology school of thought. Applied kinesiology deals with the links between muscle strength, organs, glands and the meridians of the body and uses this information to create a diagnostic muscle test. One of the students, Dr. Roger Callahan, further expounded on Applied Kinesiology by developing an approach known as TFT or Thought Field Therapy.

This therapy is still used today, and is based on 14 meridian points. These points are stimulated by lightly tapping upon them in a certain order and sequence diagnosed through individual muscle testing. One of Dr Callahan's students, Gary Craig took this therapy to completely new levels ten years ago, in 1996, when he had the bright idea to create a very simple technique that covered all 14 meridian points by default. This further aided the therapy by eliminating the need for extensive muscle testing and diagnostic training that was needed for TFT.

The therapy is known as EFT TM or the Emotional Freedom Technique and is one of the easiest, most effective and more efficient therapies that have emerged. It offers fast, effective and often permanent relief for a wide variety of psychological, physical and neurophysiologic maladies. In fact, it has been referred to as one of the most important breakthroughs in mind –body healing to have occurred in the last century!

Even more attractive EFT was designed in such a way that once you've been able to learn the simple technique, you can use it at home, at work, anywhere, anytime you need it-without further training or investing years of your life in study. New insights and training in the field of new energy therapies can be found with the Association for Meridian Therapies ((AMT) – an organization created in 1998 to help offer new insights and training in the field of these new energy therapies. Energy healing is a life long journey which means that one must keep on learning and absorbing information.

Learning to focus on your Client instead of yourself- Sometimes, it is hard to let go of yourself and give yourself over to someone else. This is especially true in instances where your own intuition may bring to light a blockage or situation that your client might not be quiet ready to address.

THE DIFFERENCE BETWEEN ADVANCED AND REGULAR ENERGY HEALING?

Aside from the mental, emotional and spiritual demands that advanced energy healing will place upon you are some additional differences between practicing energy healing and mastering it. One of the most pronounced differences is the capacity to train others to become adept too. While it's standard practice to equip your clients with a deeper understanding of their imbalances and how to promote healing within themselves, that's quite a bit different from training them to heal others.

In many styles of energy healing, it's a requirement that you first achieve mastery status yourself before you can begin training the novices. Of course, a byproduct of this tendency often means that in order to learn and acquire the keys to advance energy healing, you may have to spend a good deal of your own time studying in person with a particular master or guru of your preferred style of energy healing.

Indeed, many advanced healers have training and experience greater than or equal to that of many practicing medical doctors. However, it isn't our goal to overwhelm you here, instead we're going to introduce a few relatively simple advanced techniques that will help strengthen and accelerate your healing capacity. Each of these techniques can be used either on their own or in conjunction with

other therapies.

THE PASSING OF THE HANDS

Prior to beginning the practice of passing the hands, you should start by drawing in the energy. *Here is how*:

Take a moment to collect yourself. Close your eyes and begin "seeing" and feeling the energy begin to flow into you from all directions and deep within your body. Continue "seeing" the energy as it fills your body. Feel it flow into your shoulders down into your arms and to your hands. Imagine that your hands are filling with energy, much like you might imagine water filling up a glove. Allow this energy to build in your hands, but without forcing it. Relinquish yourself to the energy. NOW YOU ARE READY TO BEGIN!!

Start out by passing your hands over (now on) the client's body in an effort to gain some clues about the condition of their energy system. Do this by moving your hands over the front of the body, with open palms about four or five inches away. Do this using one hand at a time, working from the head down to the feet. Keep your hands relaxed and leave yourself open to sensations you might otherwise ignore or overlook. Pay attention to what you feel and what impressions you receive.

✓ Do you notice any disturbances?

✓ Did you find any areas of weakness?

✓ Are your hands drawn to any region in particular?

Make note of any area that looks as though they may need some extra attention. Don't disregard any intuitive that you may "pick up on." As an additional benefit, many patients or clients find this "diagnostic" exercise quite soothing and relaxing. After you complete this portion of the exercise, it's time to begin some touch treatments. These treatments involve special hand positions which you'll use to conduct energy to the chakras. This portion of the therapy should be done while the client lies down on their back on a standard massage treatment table3. You'll begin with the 7th (Crown) chakra and work your way down to the 1st (Base) chakra.

Pay close attention to the positioning of your hands. Remember to keep your hands open and flat, keeping your fingers together yet relaxed. And don't use pressure. Whatever position you're in, remain open and aware of the energy flow. There is no set time limit to each position, though usually each area will need roughly three to five minutes worth of attention. However, the standard is to channel the energy to your client, treating each area until you notice the flow "closing itself off, or you intuitively feel that this area has "completed" its work.

Following are some hand positions and treatments for each of the 7 chakras:

7th Chakra

Place yourself at the head of the table. Now place your hands on. The crown chakra is larger than the others and this positioning allows for maximum stimulation. However, be careful not to splay your hands to far apart. Ideally, the pinkie fingers of each hand should be no more than three inches apart. You are now ready to transmit your energy to the seventh chakra.

6th Chakra

For this exercise, you will need to situate yourself on the side of the table most prefer working from the right side. Start out by centering your right hand between (but just above) the eyebrows. With your left hand, place your palm beneath the head centering it right between the back of the head and the neck. You will conduct the energy to the chakra with both of your hands.

5TH Chakra

To treat the fifth chakra, place the palm of your right hand on the center, or just above the center of the pit of the throat. Use your other hand beneath the neck, cradling it directly beneath the right hand. Now allow the energy to flow and heal.

4th Chakra

For the fourth chakra, begin by centering the palm of your right hand directly between the breast, with your left hand held along the side of your right and just above it, so that they overlap gently (just the thumbs, or at max, the thumbs and index fingers.)

3rd Chakra

You will work the solar plexus chakra by centering the palm of your right hand at the halfway point between the bottom of the sternum and belly-button. You'll find your hand resting several inches above the navel. Now, put your left hand on top of the right hand, where they gently overlap like they did in the previous treatment. Now conduct the energy.

2nd Chakra

To treat the second chakra, center your right palm, half way between your client's belly-button and front portion of thon top of the public bone (it protrudes). Overlap the left on top of the right hand as before and begin conducting the energy.

1st Chakra

When working with a client, you must treat the base chakra differently due to the fact that the first chakra is located in the genital region. Fortunately, you can still treat this chakra indirectly. Do this by placing your hands, on top of your client's hands while concentrating on visualizing and directing your energy to the chakra via the hands.

ENDING THE TREATMENT

Once you have finished working the first chakra, take a moment by yourself to help stop the energy flow. Remember to close both you and your client's chakras to avoid energy depletion.

COLOR THERAPY:

Integrating color into your healing is a powerful way to increase effectiveness.

CHAKRA AND COLOR:

7th (Crown) Violet

6th (3rd Eye) Indigo

5TH (Throat) Blue

4th (Heart) Green

3rd (Solar Plexus) Yellow

2nd (Spleen) Orange

1st (Base) Red

While you are performing the various hand positions, attempt to check the color of the chakras by observing (first in your mind's eye) the subtle color hue on the skin of the back of your own hand as you treat each chakra. The color that you "see" on the back of your hand is the reflection of your patient's energy from the chakra field. You can hone the ability by performing an intuitive reading. Concentrate briefly on the skin on the back of your right hand (which happens to be centered above the chakra) during the active, transmission phrase.

Then glance away while releasing yourself into the receptive phase. You can aid this by continuing to "see" the skin on the back of your hand, but there may also be the impression of color strong or weak, dark or discolored, on the surface of the skin of your hand. Now look again at the top of your right hand to confirm the color you saw in your mind's eye. The tone of that chakra's color will appear to you as subtle, but still discernible color, first in your mind's eye, and then later with your actual physical eyes.

THE HEALING LIGHT

For many people, it's a natural reaction to both integrating light into your healing process. Again, as with color therapy, we aren't talking about the lighting in your room, but the gentle healing light of your mind. Many healers have noticed amazing results after they begin using the visualization of light into their healing therapies.

TAPPING INTO THE HEALING LIGHT

Start out by visualizing a cloud of light beneath your hands. Try to visualize this light in your mind's eye as either a pale white, or a pale blush-white light (whichever of these seem to feel the most natural). While imagining the light, don't try to visualize it as though it's coming from your hands instead imagine it as a layer of light that surrounds your hands, with an illuminated cloud just below your palms. Now visualize this healing light flowing into your client's body this is the art of conducting the healing light. One of the hardest parts of this exercise is both visualizing and healing all at the same time. Open yourself up to the energy you need while healing at the same time you are imagining the cloud of light.

BECOMING A PROFESSIONAL HEALER

1. **TAKE A HONEST LOOK AT YOURSELF**. Part of the process of learning to identify problems in the energy system of others is to first gain a deeper understanding of your own energy system.

2. **BEST INDICATOR OF OUR OWN ENERGY SYSTEMS**. Your emotions are the best indicatory of energy. By gaining a deeper insight into your own emotional awareness, you'll get better and better at keeping your own energy state at an optimal level for healing others. Be honest when it comes to your

personal strengths and weaknesses when it comes to healing

3. **STUDY THE PRINCIPLES OF ENERGY HEALING**. Seek our books, classes and articles and anything else you can find on the topic o f energy healing. Study the principles.

4. **STUDY THE PRACTICE OF ENERGY HEALING**. This includes various styles, techniques and tools that are used in the practice of energy "maintenance."

5. **LEARN HOW TO SENSE ENERGY**. Immerse yourself in the study and mastery of

accurately reading the energy of both yourself and others. Spend a great deal of time "meditating" on the chakras of the energy system, any aura perceptions and of course, learning to employ (and pay close attention to your own innate intuition.

6. **MASTER THE ART OF ENERGY HEALING**. Practice the techniques of energy healing you have acquired on friends and relatives until you're comfortable enough to begin healing actual "client" on a professional basis. Maintain treatment files on each person you see and keep written notes on treatments, progress reports and suggested

recommendations for the client to complete while away from your treatment facility.

7. **BRUSH UP ON BUSINESS SKILLS**. Book and record keeping. Create calm, soothing environment wher3e you can treat your clients. Create templates for your anticipated standard forms, agreements and documents.

8. **MARKETING PLAN**. Radio air time, classified ad and mail out press releases never forget that your marketing efforts will play out a decisive role in your professional success.

BECOME A GREAT ENERGY
HEALER THE TIME IS RIGHT
AND THE TIME IS NOW!!!!

Learn More **TODAY** at
http://www.thekeystowisdom.c
om